Lucy Loses Her Tonsils

NIGEL SNELL

Hamish Hamilton · London

Lucy lived in an old farmhouse
with her mummy and daddy
and baby brother and a large
soft penguin.

But her mummy was worried.

Lucy had another sore throat

d so did her penguin!

Lucy's Mummy decided to take Lucy
to the doctor.

He asked her to say Ahhhhh . . .
so he could see her tonsils.

The doctor shook his head. "Those will have to come out," he said. "I'll arrange for Lucy to go to hospital."

Lucy told her penguin he would have to come too . . .

he wasn't very keen.

Two weeks later Mummy took Lucy to the town and into the hospital—it was very big! In the nurse's office Lucy was weighed, and had a label with her name on it stuck round her arm.

She put one round penguin's flipper as well.

Then a very kind nurse took Lucy
to a ward with lots and lots of toys
and a large TV set.

She was popped into a big bed
and soon a doctor came.
He took her temperature and
listened to her chest.
(It tickled a bit!)

In the next bed was anoth[er]
little girl called Mary,
and all down the ward
there were more boys and
girls laughing and playing

In the distance, Lucy could see
the nurse bringing round a
lovely supper.
Lucy suddenly felt quite hungry.

Next morning she was
put into a long
white gown. Lucy was not
allowed to have any
breakfast . . .

. . . but a large kind nurse gave her some syrup to make her feel sleepy.

She was put on a little trolley, and a man with a big smile took her to another room. When Lucy arrived there, a lady doctor asked her to try and blow up a large red balloon till it burst.
She puffed and puffed and puffed . . .

. . . . and got sleepier
and sleepier,
and sleepier.

She dreamed that all her toys had come to see her, and were jumping up and down on her bed and playing games.

When Lucy woke up she still had a sore throat but the doctor said that her tonsils had gone and she would soon feel better. Later that day Mummy and Daddy came in to see her.

For the first day Lucy was only
allowed to eat jelly and ice cream.
She didn't mind at all!!!

Her penguin was glad
when they got home later
that week, as he only
really liked fish.

Hardback edition first published in Great Britain 1978 by
Hamish Hamilton Children's Books
Garden House, 57-59 Long Acre, London WC2E 9JZ
Copyright©1978 by Nigel Snell
All Rights Reserved

Reprinted 1982, 1983

Paperback edition first published 1984

ISBN 0-241-89920-6 (hardback)
ISBN 0-241-11192-7 (paperback)

Printed in Great Britain by
Cambus Litho, East Kilbride